THE 4S HANDBOOK

Selective Sound Sensitivity Syndrome

Duncan Alexander McKenzie R.N.

Sniffing, Gulping, Lip smacking, Loud chewing, Jaw clicking, Noisy breathing, Slurping, Licking fingers.

Aaaaaarrrgggghhh!

When Hell is the noises that other people make!

The 4S Handbook

ISBN 978-1-105-72759-7

Table of Contents

Introduction

'I can't sit through anything if someone is breathing loud, chewing loudly, smacking their lips, talking with a mouth full of food, drumming their fingers, or swinging their foot. It drives me insane. It has for a while, and it gets worse as time goes on. I'm not joking when I say I want to strangle or physically harm someone when they do any of the things mentioned above.'(1)

'I too can't stand the noise of people eating, slurping, lip smacking and especially chewing ice and hard stuff. It makes me cringe and makes me feel like I could get really aggressive. I'm 23 years old and have had it since a teenager and it has only gotten worse.' (2)

There are certain individuals on this planet, and the author of this book is one of them, who live a nightmare. This nightmare occurs every day, and it can occur in any place where there are other people. The triggering sounds can lead to anger, frustration, rage, depression and isolation. The condition has led to relationships breaking up. It has led to physical assaults. It has resulted in the loss of employment. It may have even led in at least one case to homicide. The nightmare has a name: 4S, or Selective Sound Sensitivity Syndrome. A syndrome is a specific group of symptoms that collectively indicate or characterize a disease, psychological disorder, or other abnormal condition. For those individuals who do not suffer from 4S it may seem a strange malady. Why on Earth, one might ask, would someone get so upset about certain sounds? Sounds that everyone makes from time to time. Sounds that are essentially harmless. All of us from time to time sniff, clear our throats, smack our lips and noisily suck our fingers after eating that sticky cake that tasted so delicious. These are the harmless sounds that occur every day and are made by humans in the course of their daily life. There are some lucky individuals who are completely unaffected by such sounds. They can relax in public places, with the family, in restaurants, on planes and with anyone else in a confined space and simply enjoy the company of those present. They can concentrate on what is being said, or remain engrossed in a book, and not worry about such things. Noises that other people make may seem to them at worst trivial distractions. The 4S sufferer has a different experience. Such sounds are excruciating to hear, and invoke the strongest of emotional reactions. Life can become a nightmare and serious social and occupational dysfunction may occur. The 4S syndrome is poorly understood by scientists and researchers. Indeed, even though it affects many people it has only relatively recently, along with the current trend to medicalize everything, gained a place as a syndrome in its own right. It truly deserves this place as a separate clinical entity, as it has different characteristics and symptoms that prevent it being understood in the framework of other conditions.

In this book we are going to explore the 4S syndrome and attempt to understand it better. I hope it will bring some hope to the sufferer and allow them to understand that they are not alone. We will a little later define 4S, and in writing about any medical or psychological condition we must also discuss facts such as the *incidence* and the *prevalence* of the disease, which are common terms used when discussing the epidemiology of a syndrome. Incidence is the rate of new (or newly diagnosed) cases of the disorder. It is generally reported as the number of new cases occurring within a period of time (e.g., per month, per year). It is more meaningful when the incidence rate is reported as a fraction of the population at risk of developing the disease (e.g., per 100,000 or per million population). Obviously, the accuracy of incidence data depends upon the accuracy of diagnosis and reporting of the disease. Incidence rates can be further categorized according to different subsets of the population. For example by gender, by racial origin, by age group or by diagnostic category. Prevalence is the actual number of cases alive with the disease either during a period of time (period prevalence) or at a particular date in time (point prevalence). Prevalence is also most meaningfully reported as the number of cases as a fraction of the total population at risk and can be further categorized according to different subsets of the popula-tion.(3) What do we know about the incidence and prevalence of 4S? Unfortunately there has been very little clinical research and clinical studies undertaken, and therefore we know very little about its incidence and prevalence. We know from anecdotal accounts that the condition is actually quite common; it is by no means a rare disorder. There is a need for much greater research. We need to ask questions such as if there are any cultural variations in the disorder, that is are certain racial groups less likely to suffer from 4S. And if so, why? We need to ask what the specific protective factors are in people that do not develop the disorder. We need to find out more about a genetic link. If there is a genetic link then in the future it may well be possible to identify the gene responsible.

Like other disorders of this type support and understanding from other people can make the difference between a life of isolation and distress, and one in which the sufferer has an understanding of their condition and can effectively cope with it. They can also have the reassurance that what they experience is experienced by others too. That they are not 'freaks' or 'crazy', as some have been labeled by people who do not have, and do not understand, the disorder. So let us now embark on our journey. A journey in which we hope to understand a little more about 4S, what its symptoms are, who is afflicted, and what interventions there may be available. The lives of those who suffer from the 4S syndrome are blighted by a condition that is poorly understood, and for which there is little clinical research and no clear effective treatment. There is certainly not at this point in time any claims to there being an effective cure for the syndrome. And so it is important that sufferers, and their relatives and friends, have information available to them that can help them understand the condition. This information, this support and auxiliary therapeutic interventions, which will be described later, will be the key to allowing the sufferer to cope with the condition. For the 4S sufferer intervention is aimed at utilizing effective coping strategies. I hope this book will assist the sufferer to understand their condition better, and help them feel less isolated. I hope too that it will also assist health care professionals and relatives to understand what this syndrome is about, so that they can help and support the sufferer of the disorder that we refer to as 4S.

1

The history of the 4S syndrome

In the 1980s, a clinician by the name of Dr. Pawel Jastreboff noticed such cases as described in the introduction above, and began to report on them over time. The term *misophonia* was coined to represent this condition. At the same time, Dr. Marsha Johnson, an audiologist, was also identifying similar cases and chose the term selective sound sensitivity syndrome, or soft sound sensitivity syndrome, which was shortened to 4S over time.(1) An audiologist is a health-care professional specializing in the identifying, diagnosing, treating and the monitoring of disorders of the auditory and vestibular system portions of the ear.(2) Individuals who had 4S would have initiated contact or have been referred to Dr. Johnson, under the belief that the syndrome may have been related to a disorder in the physical process of hearing. It became apparent to Dr. Johnson over time that there existed a group of individuals who displayed no physical or organic hearing conditions, however were emotionally distressed by certain noises, referred to as 'soft sounds'; natural noises that other people made in the course of eating or breathing. The pattern of their symptomatology was clear. The sufferers displayed consistent reactions, what may be termed 'sensitivity reactions' to specific sounds, hence the term 'selective sound sensitivity syndrome', or 4S. Dr Johnson determined that these individuals formed a specific population and that their symptoms were different from the other recognized syndromes relating to hearing known at that time. Prior to the establishment of the 4S syndrome as a clinical syndrome in its own right, it was considered as being associated with other syndromes. These included:

Phonophbia. Literally a fear of sounds. It can relate to specific sounds, or specific tones or pitches of sound.(3) It may also be called *'noise anxiety'*, and also has been called *'noise phobia'*. In my view 4S shares some of the characteristics of a phobia, however it has individual characteristics, or symptoms, of its own and therefore 4S is best understood as an individual clinical entity. A phobia (from the Greek *phobos* meaning "fear" or "morbid fear") is, when used in the context of clinical psychology, a type of anxiety disorder, usually defined as a persistent fear of a specific object or situation which the sufferer commits to great lengths in avoiding. The response is disproportional to the actual danger posed, and it is recognized by the sufferer as being irrational. In the event the phobia cannot be avoided entirely the sufferer will endure the situation or object with marked distress and it can cause significant interference in social or occupational activities.(4)

Hearing Loss with Recruitment. In this syndrome a person has significant hearing loss with cochlear damage and nerve damage. Thus there is an organically based etiology, or cause, of the syndrome. The sound sensitivity is referred to as recruitment. This is an abnormal growth of loudness where a tone cannot be heard due to hearing loss until it reaches a certain loudness, then it becomes rapidly very loud rather than the normally gradual linear increase in loudness experienced by normal hearers.(5)

Sensory integration dysfunction. This is a neurological disorder characterized by a neurological sensory integration deficit. The more current diagnostic nosology (Miller et al., 2007) uses the term *sensory processing disorder* to describe this condition.(6) Sensory integration dysfunction was first studied in-depth by Anna Jean Ayres. Ayres describes sensory integration as the ability to organize sensory information for use by the brain. An individual with sensory integration dysfunction would therefore have an inability to organize sensory information as it comes in through the senses. Along with sensory processing dysfunction, the term sensory integration dysfunction is used informally in the medical literature to describe any such difficulty. Various conditions can invoke sensory integration dysfunction, such as schizophrenia, succinic semialdehyde dehydrogenase deficiency, prenatal alcohol exposure, learning difficulties, autism, as well as traumatic brain injury.(7) 4S has no association with sensory integration dysfunction.

Hyperacusis. Hyperacusis (also spelled *hyperacousis*) is a health condition characterized by an over-sensitivity to certain frequency ranges of sound (a collapsed tolerance to normal environmental sound). A person with severe hyperacusis has difficulty tolerating everyday sounds, some of which may seem unpleasantly loud to that person but not to others.(8) People with hyperacusis may find that certain sounds are more difficult to listen to than others. Some sounds may cause pain in the ears, even when those sounds do not affect others. Often, the most disturbing or painful sounds can be sudden high pitched noises like alarms, bus brakes, silverware and dishes, children's screams, and clapping. Many sounds that were previously perceived as normally loud or non intrusive, can be painful, annoying, seem amplified, or prove to be irritating to the sufferer. The syndrome can be acquired as a result of damage sustained to the hearing apparatus, or inner ear. By far the most common causes of hyperacusis are noise injuries and head injuries. There is speculation that the efferent portion of the auditory nerve (*olivocochlear bundle*) has been affected (*efferent* meaning fibers that originate in the brain which serve to regulate sounds). This theory suggests that the efferent fibers of the auditory nerve are selectively damaged, while the hair cells that allow the hearing of pure tones in an audiometric evaluation remain intact. In cases not involving aural trauma to the inner ear, hyperacusis can also be acquired as a result of damage to the brain or the neurological system. It can also be caused by an adverse reaction to certain medications, especially those which principally affect the central nervous system. Other causes include chronic ear infections or autoimmune conditions.(9) In some cases the condition is idiopathic, that is, there is simply no immediately discernable cause. Hyperacusis can be defined as a cerebral processing problem specific to how the brain perceives sound. In rare cases, hyperacusis may be caused by a vestibular disorder. This type of hyperacusis, called vestibular hyperacusis, is caused by the brain perceiving certain sounds as motion input as well as auditory input. Those with 4S tolerate louder sounds very well and most often do not have hyperacusis.(10)

    Social phobia. Social phobias typically appear in childhood or adolescence, sometimes following an upsetting or humiliating experience. Certain vulnerable children who have had unpleasant social experiences (such as being rejected) or who have poor social skills may develop social phobias. The condition also may be related to low self-esteem, unassertive personality, and feelings of inferiority.(11) Advances in neuroimaging have also led researchers to identify certain parts of the brain and specific neural pathways that are associated with phobias such as social phobia. One part of the brain that is currently being studied is the *amygdala*, an almond-shaped body of nerve cells involved in normal fear conditioning. The *amygdala* is an almond shaped mass of nuclei located deep within the temporal lobe of the brain. It is a limbic system structure that is involved in many of our emotions and motivations, particularly those that are related to survival. The *amygdala* is involved in the processing of emotions such as fear, anger and pleasure. It is also responsible for determining what memories are stored, and where the memories are stored in the brain. It is thought that this determination is based on how huge an emotional response an event invokes. The *amygdala* is involved in several functions of the body including: arousal, autonomic responses associated with fear, emotional responses, hormonal secretions and memory.(12)

Misophonia. This term literally means a dislike of sounds. A wide spectrum of sounds and noise can cause the sufferer to feel great distress and to isolate themselves from noisy environments. The sufferer experiences the sensation of *sensory overload.* Sufferers frequently resort to the use of ear plugs to block out all sound, and the syndrome can have significant impact on the individual's life and day to day functioning. The treatment for *misophonia* is based on the work of Dr. Pawel and Margaret Jastreboff and needs to be administered by specifically trained medical providers. Clinically, 4S has been classified as a subset of the *misophonia* classification. The sufferers in this group have specific characteristics with regards to their hearing. Those with 4S mostly are able to tolerate louder sounds very well and on clinical examination by an audiologist there are no symptoms of hyperacusis or recruitment.(13)

The above information is useful to allow us to firstly define what exactly the 4S syndrome is, and allow us to clarify its classification in the spectrum of other hearing disorders. At this point in our discussion of 4S we have therefore determined that 4S has special characteristics of its own. Its constellation of symptoms distinguishes it from other clinical entities and groupings of symptoms. The branch of medicine that deals with the classification of diseases is referred to as *'nosology'*.(14)

Our sense of hearing is a magical thing. To hear the birds singing in the trees, greeting us with their enchanting melodies. To hear someone say "I love you." To hear the music of Beethoven or Vivaldi. Such sensory experiences can take us to the gates of Heaven. However sufferers of 4S are often taken to the gates of Hell. Every day. At work, at home, wherever they are with other people. We cannot avoid other people completely. We often cannot avoid eating with them. We cannot avoid sitting on a long haul plane trip being forced to listen to someone clearing the particles of peanuts he has just eaten from between his teeth. At these times 4S sufferers will curse that they can hear at all, and will fantasize about throwing the other passenger off the plane. Without a parachute! Then they will feel terrible guilty, because for the most part 4S sufferers are nice people and really don't want to harm anyone at all. They just want peace and to be able to sit and to relax and enjoy other people's company, just like anyone else.

For the vast majority of 4S sufferers there is no organic pathology that can be found to explain the condition. No structural problems with their brains, no structural or functional problems with their hearing. They are essentially otherwise completely normal people.

I mentioned Beethoven above. And I mentioned the fact that sometimes 4S sufferers, so tortured as they are by the trigger noises that so upset them, often wish they could not hear. But then they would not be able to hear Beethoven's wonderful music that has so enchanted us. For clinicians, and any others who are interested in such matters, Beethoven started to lose his hearing at the age of 28 years. By the age of forty four years his hearing loss was complete, and pathologists have stated that based on the information available it is most likely this was caused by compression of the eighth cranial nerve caused by Paget's disease. This is a bone disease that can result in enlarged and misshapen bones. This disease affected his skull. The *vestibulocochlear nerve* (auditory vestibular nerve) is the eighth of twelve cranial nerves, and is responsible for transmitting sound and equilibrium (balance) information from the inner ear to the brain.(15) After Beethoven's death an autopsy on his body was performed in Vienna on March 27, 1827 by the famous pathologist Dr. Rokitansky. Dr. Rokitansky identified a uniformly dense skull vault and thick and shriveled auditory nerves, consistent with Paget's disease of bone. Further investigation showed no evidence of syphilitic arthritis (inflammation of the arteries caused by syphilis) in the auditory arteries or of recurrent *otitis media*, or middle ear infection. The liver, however, was atrophic, nodular, and cirrhotic. Beethoven died of alcoholic liver disease, the result of alcohol misuse by a musician whose progressive hearing loss led to depression. Hearing was the sense Beethoven required more than any other. His love of music was a powerful force, preventing him from committing suicide. Much of his great music flowed from the mind of a man who never heard its beauty. He used an ear trumpet that he secured with a headband, leaving his hands free for conducting.(16) This sad tale will remind us to treasure our wonderful sense of hearing, and to hope that we can cope with 4S and manage our symptoms effectively. Then life will be bearable, and we will still have the option to listen to life's sweet sounds.

2

My story as a 4S sufferer

I am a Registered Nurse. I am also a 4S sufferer. The reason that I mention this is so the reader does not feel that this book is simply a clinical treatise, or that I am viewing their suffering from a cold, clinical point of view. I myself have the symptoms of 4S and so I have lived and I have experienced the suffering that goes with this condition. As so typically occurs with this disorder the symptoms in my own case developed during early adolescence. During the age when sound doesn't seem to matter. I was twelve year old. When one runs about and shouts and has the TV on loud and listens to pop music at jet engine decibel level. As I get older I find that my general tolerance for noise has decreased. Now in my 50's I yearn for 'peace and quiet' and actually enjoy the music that one hears in elevators. Now that is really diagnostic that one is getting old! So the contradiction is that with 4S the syndrome typically commences at a time in our lives when we really don't mind sound and noise in general at all. It seems to much less frequently begin in our older years, the years when one would imagine we are much less tolerant of sound. I can actually remember the time that I first experienced its symptoms, and from then on it has exerted its power over me and has never let go. I loved my parents. My mother was a wonderful woman who was full of life and gave my sisters and I a loving home. She was very 'house-proud', and we lived in a spotlessly clean working class home. She had obsessional traits, but never suffered from obsessional disorder in any acute form. One evening my parents had some friends over and I was sitting next to my mother as everyone engaged in general conversation. My mother loved to have cups of tea regularly during the day, and this evening everyone sat with drinks and my mum with her usual cuppa. Then she took a mouthful of tea and swallowed. The normal sound of another person swallowing is an innocent and barely perceptible sound. But to me it sounded like a big gulp, and for some unfathomable reason I became immediately aware of her gulp, and felt a sense of annoyance. I felt irritated and my cognition was very much caught up in that sound. From that time on things got rapidly worse. My father was an ex-military, no nonsense man, who brought my sisters and I up very strictly. He had a habit of smacking his lips after he had eaten. I had never noticed it before, but it started to really annoy me. This got to the point where I was simply not able to sit and eat my meals with other members of the family. This hyper vigilance that I had, this sensitivity to these harmless noises that no one else seemed affected by, grew and I really did not understand what was going on. I began to eat on my own. With my food on a tray, in my bedroom or in the living room if everyone else was in the kitchen. That was my earliest coping strategy in dealing with 4S. The use of avoidance. It is a strategy that has no therapeutic effect. It simply allows one to cope. Of course I and no one else knew that I had 4S. It was simply unheard of as a discrete syndrome at that time. One time I had to sit at the table and eat with my family. Hearing the noises of them eating was torture. I wanted to escape, to run, to cry, to shout out, "stop eating like pigs!" One time it got so bad I actually told my father "you eat like a pig!" I was young and did not have the skills to communicate effectively and in a non-threatening way. I should have said, "I'm sorry but there is something wrong with me. For some reason I get very distressed by certain noises that people make. It's not your fault, and it's not my fault. I have no control over these reactions that I have." My father responded to my verbal tirade naturally with anger. And the situation continued where there was no alternative but for me to avoid eating meals with my family. What a miserable situation. Having to isolate oneself from one's family. That was over forty years ago and the symptoms have never abated. The same old reactions of rage are there. For me the trigger noises are lip smacking, sucking on food that is stuck in one's teeth, noisily licking one's fingers after eating with the hands, eating food with one's mouth open, sniffing and loud breathing through the nose. The experience can be particularly bad on public transport. Being stuck on a train or a bus there is always someone who is sniffing constantly, or loudly chewing gum. It is particularly bad when the sounds are behind me. As is common, apart from the dreadful physical sensations that one experiences when one hears these sounds, one is beset with violent fantasies regarding the person who is making the noises. I have never in all of my years of suffering from the disorder actually strangled anyone, but I have fantasized about doing so countless times! 4S sufferers may well say to people who happen to annoy them, "Hi! I just saved your life!" The person no doubt on being so addressed would respond in a surprised manner, "Saved my life? How exactly?" The 4S sufferer would respond by saying "I could have strangled you, but didn't!" From time to time, if there is someone who is making the trigger sounds particularly badly, I may get really annoyed and upset. It may be someone who is eating fried chicken legs with their mouths open, smacking their lips in satisfaction at the taste, licking their greasy fingers noisily, and then once finished with the food, sucking noisily to get the chicken particles out from between their teeth. In such situations I have been known to give the person a nasty stare. The poor individual would probably wonder why I am doing that. They would probably nudge their partner, who is sitting next to them happily looking out the train window without the slightest hint of annoyance at this noisy eater, and indicate in my direction. *Why is that guy looking at me so strangely?* I have on many occasions had to leave restaurants when it has just gotten intolerable to listen to the cacophony of lip smacking and chewing noises. It is blight on one's life, this 4S. Other people can relax. Can enjoy time with their families and friends. Can go to restaurants and cinemas and eat with everyone and not be the slightest bit affected. But the 4S sufferer is continuously on edge. Hyper vigilant and alert for the person whom they know will turn up to spoil their night. As if by magic that person will appear in the cinema, sitting right behind them despite all of the empty seats everywhere else, with a huge bucket of popcorn that will be munched noisily until we're half way through the movie. Why do movie theaters still sell that stuff? Or the 4S sufferer is enjoying a quiet commute to work on the train. It will be just about to pull away from one station, and someone will just make it on board. They sit next to you, pleased with themselves that they have just made it on board. Two minutes later. *Sniff.* Then *sniff sniff.* Then one big giant sniff where one almost hears the mucous of this person gurgling down their throat. Then they get out a cough candy. *Suck. Slurp. Sniff.* I squirm and try to move away. I get up and go over to the train station map on the wall of the train, to make it appear I am getting away from this person for a reason. I then after studying the map sit down as far away as possible from the 'offender'. On really bad days I have had to get off of the train if it is full of people and the trigger noises are just overwhelming. I find that if I am stressed about general matters, about other issues in my life, then the 4S symptoms seem worse. As everyone else who also suffers from the syndrome work can be a trial. If one works with other people that is. In my own profession, working as part of a clinical team, it is inevitable that I am regularly subject to trigger noises. Team meetings and seminars and the like can sometimes be dreaded for this reason. During a seminar someone might have the bright idea of setting out candy, pieces of fruit or peanuts on the table, just so that people could "nibble" during the proceedings. Aaarrggh! *"Beam me up, Scotty!"* As they would say on Star Trek. Unfortunately there is no way that could happen. It can be a real effort to keep focused on the proceedings and to concentrate on the content of the seminar. In my own experience there is little that can be done except to block out noise altogether, there are no remedies that I know of that will block out the specific trigger noises of 4S, and there have been no medications developed specifically for the condition. For seminars and work there is no option to use the tried and true ear plugs coping strategy. One has to suffer in silence.

There may over time be medicines that are found to be useful for the condition. Such is the history of medicine. Medications that are used to target one specific illness are found coincidentally to be effective in treating other disorders too. In the way that the drug *quinine* was used to treat malaria, but then was found to have a therapeutic effect on arthritic symptoms. This is termed a 'seren-dipitous' find. An accidental and fortunate discovery.(1) Not all groundbreaking medical discoveries by any means occur by design. Some are purely good luck, but good luck and the researcher's preparedness to follow the link. A celebrated instance of serendipity in biomedical research took place in 1928 at St Mary's Hospital in London. While studying *staphylococci* (staph bacteria), the physician and microbiologist, Sir Alexander Fleming, happened to notice that on a dish containing agar on which he had been growing germs, near some mould the germs were less common. He grew more of the mould and named it penicillin from its Latin name *Penicillium*. Fleming found the mould was effective against bacteria that caused diseases such as anthrax, meningitis and diphtheria. This heralded the age of antibiotics and a huge advance in medical treatment.(2) There may be other medications that come into clinical practice that are used to treat an unrelated condition in a 4S sufferer, and it is found coincidentally that the drug has an effect in lessening or controlling the symptoms of 4S. Or our knowledge of neuroscience may reach the point where we are finally able to elicit precisely the neurophysiologic mechanisms involved in 4S, and create from scratch a medication that specifically targets the symptoms.

For anyone who suffers from 4S it becomes apparent that the symptoms remain with the sufferer over many years, if not their whole lifetime. Certain medical conditions come and go in discrete episodes. And certain conditions occur for only one episode in the sufferer and then vanish never to return. Or their symptoms can be medically controlled. In my own case 4S has remained with me until now. A companion that never leaves me, and is always ready to rear its ugly head as soon as the right person comes along to make the trigger sounds. My own opinion is that the disorder, due to its usually early onset, is linked to faulty neuro-sensory processing in the maturing brain. The precise mechanism of this is unknown, but once it is there it becomes 'hard-wired' in to the mature neural pathways of our brains. In the primitive structures of our brain, those essentially responsible for the 'fight or flight' reaction. The frontal lobes of our brain, the areas responsible for the executive functioning, reasoning, and thinking logically have no direct control over our primitive responses such as anger and fear. We cannot turn these on and off. The 4S sufferer often feels guilty over getting angry at others, and feels that their reactions are irrational. But they are powerless to do anything about them. It is important to understand this as sometimes relatives or friends who may be on the receiving end of anger directed at them by the sufferer may feel that the sufferer is 'putting it on', or can control this behavior. The 4S sufferer has no control over the symptoms of the condition. It's just part of us, and for most of us it is not going to go away.

3

The symptoms and experiences of 4S sufferers

'I have this problem, and I think one day I am going to explode. My mom chews with her mouth open and eats crunchy food all day long. I have literally had to leave the room any time I see her make toast or pull out peanuts. I start to get uncontrollably mad when she does this and I want to hurt her when she does. I confronted her once on this and she immediately said I was crazy and that if I don't cut this out, she is going to ground me. I realized that it is only when my mom eats that I get very hostile. She cracks her knuckles and body all day too, which gives me the same rage as the food. Please, I am fifteen and I don't want to have to deal with this for the rest of my life. If anyone knows therapy for this phobia or a cure, let me know. I am afraid that I am going to go nuts soon.' (1)

'I'm 39 and have lived with this inconvenience since I was 8. I even got discharged from the Navy because of it. My divorce was caused in part by this as well. It's been a rough *life with this issue and would take a long time to explain it all but it's actually kind of nice to see I'm not the only one in the world with this issue.'(2)*

In the realm of psychology we can define an illness as 'an abnormal process in which aspects of the social, physical, emotional, or intellectual condition and function of a person are diminished or impaired compared with that person's previous condition.'(3) So by using these criteria we can clearly refer to 4S as a psychological condition. Later we will outline exactly how the condition impacts on the sufferer, and we know it can seriously interfere with and damage relationships, and interfere with one's occupational performance. The condition may also lead to secondary symptoms, such as social avoidance, depression, poor self-esteem and chronic anxiety. Therefore we must consider not only the direct effects of the condition itself, but also the consequences and related conditions that the syndrome can invoke. That is, the other dimensions to the disorder that can occur co-morbidly. Mental Health Clinicians may treat individuals who are suffering from a clinical depression. It would be entirely possible to find that, out of the many causes possible, the depression may have been triggered, or precipitated, by 4S if such is present and it is having a severe effect on the sufferer's social life, relationships and/or work.

Let us again define our terms. What exactly are we talking about when we use the term 'Selective Sound Sensitivity Syndrome (4S)' Firstly we can state that the disorder centers on auditory sensitivities. That is, sensitivities to specific sounds. One authority on the disorder defines the condition as: '.... *an intense and immediate emotional and physiological reaction (possibly rage, frustration, sadness, or panic) upon hearing certain sounds - most prominently noises associated with oral functions such as eating, breathing, chewing or other noises such as typing sounds or pencils scratch-ing.'*(4) Most common are sounds that others make such as crunching noises, chewing gum, sniffing, someone smacking their lips, licking of the fingers while someone is eating food with their hands and people sucking on food particles that are lodged between the teeth. Other repetitive noises can induce a 4S trigger reaction in sufferers, such as typing and tapping on keyboards. Taking the above definition as a working definition we can call the reaction to the trigger sounds the '4S reaction.' Let us expand on how it manifests itself and also expand on the more common emotional and behavioral reactions to the trigger noise. The population of sufferers, from what we have been able to determine anecdotally, usually first experience the symptoms between the ages of five to fifteen. It seems rare to suddenly develop the syndrome later in life. So it is mostly reported that the onset of the condition is in childhood or early adolescence. The sufferer may suddenly feel annoyed by a noise that a family member or friend is making. Over time the trigger noises may become more numerous. The fact that the condition commences in childhood or early adolescence can have significant consequences. This is the period of social development and it may force the sufferer into a behavioral pattern of socially isolating themselves as a protective mechanism, as a defense. As a child one is also in a subordinate position and it is harder to challenge or to discuss openly what is happening, and what one is experiencing. For the very young perhaps they would not be able to articulate the symptoms and experiences fully. The child may also lack the necessary assertiveness or communication skills that would allow some resolution of the matter if it is a family member engaging in behavior that triggers a 4S reaction. There do not appear to be any clear precipitants, or triggers to the disorder itself at all, although a genetic component has been suggested. The common places where one may encounter trigger noises are in the house, at the workplace, in the cinemas, at church, on planes. But of course it can occur anywhere. The worst place for the sufferer to be is in an environment that they are not able to escape from. Suddenly, at this time of onset, they experience a sudden awareness and marked annoyance and distress in relation to specific trigger sounds. As we have stated, these sounds are often centered on the sound that other people make when eating, chewing or breathing. Once so conditioned to these sounds the sufferer finds it impossible not to notice them, even though other environmental stimuli are present. The trigger sounds provoke an immediate reaction in the sufferer and it is important to understand that the reaction occurs on three different levels. There is a *physiological reaction* linked to the autonomic nervous system. The autonomic nervous system (ANS or visceral nervous system or involuntary nervous system) is the part of the peripheral nervous system that acts as a control system. It functions largely below the level of consciousness, and controls visceral functions. The ANS affects heart rate, digestion, respiratory rate, salivation, perspiration, diameter of the pupils, and other functions. All of these functions are designed to prepare the human organism for danger, and to increase chances of survival. Whereas most of its actions are involuntary, some, such as breathing, work in tandem with the conscious mind. The ANS is classically divided into two subsystems: the *parasympathetic nervous system* (PSNS) and *sympathetic nervous system* (SNS). Relatively recently, a third subsystem of neurons that have been named 'non-adrenergic and non-cholinergic' neurons (because they use nitric oxide as a neuro-transmitter) have been described and found to be integral in autonomic function, particularly in the gut and the lungs.(5) Now, in regards to the autonomic nervous system, it is that that part of our bodies that is responsible for the fundamental 'fight or flight reaction'.

The fight or flight response (also called the fight or flight or freeze response, hyper arousal, or the acute stress response) was first described by the American physiologist Dr. Walter Bradford Cannon. His theory states that animals react to threats with a general discharge of the sympathetic nervous system, priming the animal for fighting or fleeing. This response was later recognized as the first stage of a general adaptation syndrome that regulates stress responses among vertebrates and other organisms. In the human fight or flight response in prehistoric times, fight was manifested in aggressive, combative behavior and flight was manifested by fleeing potentially threatening situations, such as being confronted by a predator. In current times, these responses persist, but fight and flight responses have assumed a wider range of behaviors. For example, the fight response may be manifested in angry, argumentative behavior, and the flight response may be manifested through social withdrawal, substance abuse, and even television viewing. Males and females tend to deal with stressful situations differently. Males are more likely to respond to an emergency situation with aggression (fight), while females are more likely to flee (flight), turn to others for help, or attempt to defuse the situation – 'tend and befriend'. During stressful times, a mother is especially likely to show protective responses toward her offspring and affiliate with others for shared social responses to threat.(6)

Evolution has allowed the 'flight or fight' structures and processes to remain within us to help us adapt to our environment. Indeed without these ancient structures that mediate this response within our brain we would not be alive for very long. The reactions that we experience prepare us to deal effectively with danger. It is the same process that exists in other animal species too. In psychological conditions such as 4S the autonomic nervous system is engaged, but for purely non-threatening stimuli. Someone chewing loudly on food or smacking their lips presents no direct danger to us. Although for some reason the stimuli is misinterpreted and a cascade of response occurs, overwhelming the sufferer and making life a misery. It is therefore not adaptive, it is maladaptive. It does not resolve any problem or increase our odds of survival. It actually causes us problems. And hence its classification as a psychological disorder.

It is difficult to understand why exactly the brain misinterprets the trigger sounds that so affect a 4S sufferer and invokes a fight or flight response, and a hyper arousal of the emotional state. There is no threat to the individual through the trigger sounds. In this respect the 4S syndrome resembles a phobia. We may draw an analogy with such syndromes as 4S occurring on a psychological level, and conditions such as allergies or hypersensitivity reactions with our immune system, which occur on a purely physiological level. Allergy or hypersensitivity (type 1 allergy) is an abnormal reaction to protein substances that occur naturally. If an allergic person is exposed to these substances called allergens, the body's immune system gets ready to fight them. Just as in the preparedness induced by the 'flight or flight reaction' our immune system gets to work to prepare to contain and defeat the danger. White blood cells (B-lymphocytes) produce an antidote (antibody) against the allergen. The antibody sticks to the surface of the allergy cells. Now the body is ready to fight back the next time it is exposed to the allergen. This process is called *sensitization*. It would appear that 4S sufferers go through this process of sensitization also. After this change, there is an allergic reaction every time the body is exposed to the allergen. And for the 4S sufferer every time a trigger sound occurs. There is no actual connection between 4S and allergic or hypersensitivity reactions. I simply use it to illustrate a point that other, purely physical, complex physiological mechanisms can misinterpret stimuli as being a threat when the stimuli are actually harmless.

In a 'fight or flight' reaction, where there is a (sympathetic) autonomic nervous system response the substances that are responsible for the mediation of the response are principally the catecholamine hormones *adrenaline* and *noradrenaline*. We are a long way off actually knowing precisely what physiological mechanisms, processes and neurotransmitters are at play in 4S. Although we can use analogies to simply allow us to present the hypothesis that the 4S syndrome occurs due to a fault in the normal auditory and stimuli processing centers of the brain. These centers are directly linked with the emotional centers dealing with basic emotions such as anger, sadness, fear and rage. I previously completed some research on anxiety disorders and phobias and I found it useful to divide the symptomatology of phobic disorder into three separate dimensions. This proved useful in terms of focusing specific interventions to each dimension. Please note that 4S and phobic disorder share some similarities, such as the desire to flee the situation in which the trigger sounds are present and the use of avoidance, however clinically they are separate entities.

With 4S we can use the same model to understand what is going on.

On a *physical level* the sufferer experiences discomfort, often described as a squirming feeling, and a feeling of physically wanting to escape the situation. This parallels the phobic response in that the individual will always attempt to flee or to avoid the phobic situation or object. This is the physiological response to a noxious stimulus.

On an *emotional level* the 4S sufferer experiences strong feelings of anger, which may be intense and therefore referred to as rage. There may also be associated behavioral responses. In a phobic response the emotion is intense fear and anxiety, not rage or anger.

On a *cognitive or thinking level* the sufferer can experience aggressive fantasies towards the person who is making the trigger sounds. In rare instances, in individuals who have poor impulse control, this can even lead to assaultive behavior initiated by the sufferer. In phobic disorders, by comparison, the individual is overwhelmed with anxiety and believes that they are going to die. There is not the same sense of rage or anger that characterizes 4S.

So let us look at the experience of the sufferer in regards to the three different levels in which the 4S syndrome is experienced. The following are from a website where 4S sufferers describe their experiences.(7) I used the posts of this website to extract raw data for our purposes of describing further the syndrome and the key symptoms and behaviors. The posts occurred between the period of September, 2006 to April, 2012 and consisted of entries made by 133 individuals. It falls short of formal research as there has been no opportunity to conduct a formal structured interview with the individuals, and the content of their postings cannot be verified directly. However it appears self-evident that these individuals are clearly describing the symptoms of 4S, and thus I accept the postings as having validity. They describe the cluster of symptoms and behaviors that are evident in 4S. We are thus engaging in the type of research that is named *phenomenological research*. This is an

inductive, descriptive research approach developed from phenomenological philosophy. Its aim is to describe an experience as it is
actually lived by the person.(8) So using this raw data in the form of
the experiences of sufferers we can separate the symptoms out into
three dimensions consistent with the physical, the emotional and
the cognitive, or thinking, level.

On the physical or physiological level:

*'This relieves me to see so many people who share this con-
dition. This has been an issue for me since I was about
maybe 11. I've become so frustrated by it sometimes that I
cry. I have to leave the room whenever it happens and I sit
in my room with feelings of great agitation and anger. I
hate feeling so hostile towards people about this. Sometimes it interferes with my concentration and thought process which further aggravates me. It annoys me most with
my father, though we have a good relationship. However I
get a sense of paranoia, like he does it on purpose, which I
know he would not, I just can't help it. I wish I knew a way
to not let it bother me, or even just know what this is.'*

*'I'm so glad other people have this. I'm 16 and I cannot
stand it when my dad eats with me. When I hear him I start
to squirm and get really upset.'*

*'I'm 13 and I hate it when people eat loudly. It makes me
shiver and I go all squirmy. Especially when my broth-
er/dad eats anything it makes me sooo annoyed. I'm glad
to hear that I'm not the only one though! I probably eat
loudly but I also hate it when people chew gum really
loud...'*

On the emotional and behavioral level:

'My family thought it was just a childish thing & I would grow out of it and actually used to tease me about it, deliberately munching their food louder while I was around. **I've cried, screamed, fought, slammed doors & punched walls** *in the past over this. It affects every single part of my life, I have to think about it before I go anywhere.'*

'It's gotten so bad that I no longer sit with my family at Christmas for dinner, I eat alone upstairs & **leave the room** *whenever someone eats, even a biscuit.'*

'I travel a lot and every time I get in an airport I get in defensive mode because of all the obnoxious gum-chewers I seem to come across. Sometimes in airports people open a plastic bottle and it sounds like gum-cracking and I **turn around and give the evil eye**. *I am seriously out of control!'*

In the above post the 4S sufferer relates how he has an on-going tension and preparedness to that which they fear (hyper vigilance), and noises can be misinterpreted as trigger sounds. This invokes a behavioral reaction, in this case turning around and giving the person 'the evil eye'.

On the cognitive level:

'I know what you mean and I'm glad I'm not the only one. I have had these symptoms for over eight years and they won't go away they only seem to get worse. I can't have dinner with friends anymore since most of them tell me I

make faces at them. My parents call me rude when I try to tell them and complain that it is a lie since most of the time I have bad hearing. It can get to the point were I can tell if someone has food in their mouth even if they're in another room. My family is disgusting. They chew with their mouths open, slurp (even cold cereal!!), love to chew on ice and smack their gum around. Just thinking about it makes me cringe. It is really painful, sometimes all I can do is get up and go to my room and cry. I feel infuriated and really want to hurt them, often just imagining slamming their faces into their food. I really need to know if there is something available to at least suppress some of the pain. I can't take it anymore, I'm loosing friends because of it.'

'*I have had a problem with lip smacking for as long as I can remember. My aunt used to be the most annoying eater, she smacked like a chipmunk when she ate. I avoided her at any holiday and refused to eat or stay at my cousin's house (when I was younger). Now I have a co-worker who annoys me as well, we usually work together on jobs in construction. The last week has been slow so we sit in the office together and he burps constantly, dips tobacco and spits every 2 minutes. Also when he eats he brings a plastic bowl and scarfs it down so fast and makes the scraping sound on the bowl with his spoon. I get so upset that I want to drop the fax machine on his head (thinking maybe a slight to moderate skull fracture will silence him). I don't recall these sounds bothering me as much until now, and all I can think back to is my aunt when I was younger. Maybe it's just being stir crazy from* sitting in the office with someone for this long considering I'm not used to it.'

'I can't believe there are people like this like myself. I have had this phobia since I was 11 years old. Before then I was a happy kid with no worries about sound. I use to love my mum doing the dishes before I'd go to sleep so I knew someone was there at night. But I'm 22 years old now... and it's just getting worse. I can't eat with my girl. I can't stand her eating or even doing the dishes or even walking up stairs as I feel she is walking heavily on the floor and it annoys the hell out of me. I have no idea how to fix this problem... **sometimes it makes me so angry that I think about killing something or someone.** Or sometimes I'll just yell words to anyone with out even realizing I am saying it. I'm in serious trouble with this.. because I'm at a stage now that it's just getting worse and worse. I really need help! You have no idea how much help I need.'

'I have had this problem since I was 7 years old. I'm 17 now.. and it keeps getting worse. First it was only chewing gum that annoyed me. Now it's food. And it's not just the sound.. **if I look at my mom and she's eating I will feel like killing her.** It sounds scary but it's almost as if Satan comes over my body or something. I'm such a laid back person that it scares people when this happens. I've been to a mental hospital and therapy and nothing helps.'

'I am so glad that I am not alone too. I can remember smacking sounds annoy me since I was about 3 or 4 yrs old. The sound of people sniffling in class also causes extreme anger and anxiety. My family has made fun of me *for years about it and it has made me feel different and alone. I am now 27 yrs of age. I've been married for 4 yrs. It seems that every since mid-way through this pregnancy my husband's breathing drives me absolutely crazy.* **I picture myself ripping his nose off and throwing it.** *It reminds me of a leaky tire or something. I have to make sure both of my ears are covered when sleeping in same bed as well. It drives me nuts. Is there anything that can cure me? I have recently switched from regular to online classes too because I can't stand the sound of people breathing or chewing gum in class.'*

'I have become extremely violent -- its almost as though I am going nuts -- I cant calm down till I have broken something. Its has gotten that bad. And to add to it my father isn't willing to help me out. The **other day my mom held onto me for almost an hour to calm me down. Its gotten that worse. I almost imagine pulling my dad's tongue out and hacking it or maybe just chopping his head off into tiny bits till its disappears.** *Just can explain the aggression.'*

For some sufferers with poor impulse control they actually have engaged in assault as in the following post:

'I'm one of you guys, **I have actually slammed someone's head into a wall** *for doing this after I told him his being too loud nicely...it's a problem no doubt, it can't be ignored, but I don't think it can be stopped either.'*

In at least one case a homicide has been reported as a response to what may be assumed to be an extreme behavioral reaction to someone's noisy eating. It was reported that a man was shot dead at a Latvian cinema after eating his popcorn too loudly during a movie. Police said they had arrested a 27-year-old man suspected of shooting a 42-year-old fellow audience member who later died of his wounds. The conflict took place as the credits rolled during the screening of a movie, according to police in the Baltic state. Witnesses told the Latvian news agency Leta that the argument arose over how loudly the deceased man was eating his popcorn. The shooting occurred on Saturday evening in the central multiplex cinema in the Latvian capital, Riga. Gun-crime is relatively rare in Latvia, a European Union nation of 2.2 million. The shooter reportedly was a graduate of the police academy and held a doctorate in law from the University of Latvia.(9)

Fortunately actual assault and actual homicide are rare, however one may see in the courts for those charged perhaps a legal defense based on 4S being a recognized syndrome. Thus a medical defense. Despite this we hope that the courts determine those who have committed acts of violence as guilty. Having 4S does not diminish the responsibility that sufferers have to others, and to live as law abiding citizens. However hard at times that may be!

4

The anatomy and physiology of hearing

In view of the fact that 4S relates to the uncontrollable and mala-daptive response to certain harmless sounds let us examine the process of hearing. Again let me stress that the majority of 4S sufferers do not suffer from any pathology of the hearing organs or any clear demonstrable brain pathology. However it is very important to remember that should you experience any symptoms relating to your hearing a visit to your family doctor and a general check-up would be in order. This would also allow your doctor to monitor your condition, to provide general support and any referral to other health professionals, such as audiologists, that may be necessary. And medicine is a two way street. Doctors and nurses and health professionals learn from their patients and if your doctor hasn't heard about 4S then it's about time he or she did!

The mechanism of hearing is a miracle of biological design and engineering. The auditory system can be viewed as being divided into distinct anatomical entities:

The outer ear

The folds of cartilage surrounding the ear canal are called the *pinna*. Sound waves are reflected and attenuated when they hit these folds. These changes provide additional information that will help the brain determine the direction from which the sounds came. In an evolutionary sense this had important functions in terms of locating prey or of locating any source of sound that may present a threat. The sound waves enter the auditory canal, a deceptively simple tube. The ear canal amplifies sounds that are between 3 and 12 kHz. At the far end of the ear canal is the eardrum (or *tympanic membrane*), which marks the beginning of the middle ear. Certain species of animals have extraordinarily acute hearing. The owl is one example. They have larger ear holes that can pinpoint a mouse or other small prey and they can quickly, within .01 of a second, access its distance. Since bats hunt at night, they have echolocation like dolphins. They can locate insects from 20 feet away. When considering such animal wonders such as these one can also understand the experience of the 4S sufferer who is also hyper vigilant in regards to trigger noises and can locate them from afar. It is also important to understand how hearing and its mechanisms developed in the context of evolution and survival of the species. However the mystery in regards to 4S is 'what possible survival advantage could there be to being aware of and reacting to someone smacking their lips?' Is it possible that attentiveness to soft sounds may have offered a survival advantage? At night in a cave our prehistoric ancestors would have needed to have been aware of the soft sounds of a saber toothed tiger quietly creeping up to the cave entrance. A twig breaking, the sound of a low pitched almost imperceptible growl, and its soft breathing. Perhaps the saber tooth tiger was licking its lips at the thought of the nice feast the cave man would present! If so, we can understand how 4S would be useful in some way. To arouse us on perceiving these noises and to get us out of the situation fast!

The middle ear

Sound waves traveling through the ear canal will hit the *tympanic membrane*, or eardrum. This wave information travels across the air-filled middle ear cavity via a series of delicate bones: the *malleus* (hammer), *incus* (anvil) and *stapes* (stirrup). These *ossicles* act as a lever and a form of teletype, converting the lower-pressure eardrum sound vibrations into higher-pressure sound vibrations at another, smaller membrane called the *oval* (or elliptical) window. The *malleus* articulates with the *tympanic membrane* via the *manubrium*, where the *stapes* articulates with the oval window via its footplate. Higher pressure is necessary because the inner ear beyond the oval window contains liquid rather than air. The sound is not amplified uniformly across the *ossicular chain*. The *stapedius reflex* of the middle ear muscles helps protect the inner ear from damage. The middle ear still contains the sound information in wave form; it is converted to nerve impulses in the *cochlea*.

The inner ear

The inner ear consists of the *cochlea* and several non-auditory structures. The cochlea has three fluid-filled sections, and supports a fluid wave driven by pressure across the *basilar membrane* separating two of the sections. One section, called the *cochlear duct* or *scala media*, contains *endolymph*, a fluid similar in composition to the intracellular fluid found inside cells. The *organ of Corti* is located in this duct on the basilar membrane, and this is responsible for the transformation of mechanical waves into electric signals in neurons. The other two sections are known as the *scala tympani* and the *scala vestibuli*. These are located within the *bony labyrinth*, which is filled with fluid called *perilymph*, similar in composition to cerebrospinal fluid. The chemical difference between *endolymph* and *perilymph* is important for the function of the inner ear due to electrical potential differences between potassium and calcium ions.

The organ of Corti

The *organ of Corti* forms a ribbon of sensory epithelium which runs lengthwise down the cochlea's entire *scala media*. Its hair cells transform the fluid waves into nerve signals. From here, further processing leads to a panoply of auditory reactions and sensations.

The hair cell

Hair cells are columnar cells, each with a bundle of 100-200 specialized cilia at the top, for which they are named. There are two types of hair cells. Inner hair cells are the *mechanoreceptors* for hearing: they transduce the vibration of sound into electrical activity in nerve fibers, which is transmitted to the brain. *Outer hair cells* are a motor structure. Sound energy causes changes in the shape of these cells, which serves to amplify sound vibrations in a frequency specific manner. Resting atop the longest cilia of the inner hair cells is the *tectorial membrane*, which moves back and forth with each cycle of sound, tilting the *cilia*. This is the mechanism that elicits the hair cells electrical responses. *Inner hair cells*, like the photoreceptor cells of the eye, show a graded response, instead of the spikes typical of other neurons.

Hair cell neural connection

Afferent neurons innervate cochlear inner hair cells, at synapses where the neurotransmitter *glutamate* communicates signals from the hair cells to the dendrites of the primary auditory neurons. *Afferent* or *sensory neurons*, receive information from the outside, through sensory receptors, and sends this to other neurons so the body can produce a response. *Efferent neurons* or *motor neurons* receive information from other neurons and send that information to effectors (muscles, glands), which produce a motor or behavioral response. Many auditory nerve fibers are innervated by each hair cell. The *neural dendrites* belong to neurons of the auditory nerve, which in turn joins the vestibular nerve to form the *vestibulocochlear nerve*, or cranial nerve number VIII. Efferent projections from the brain to the cochlea also play a role in the *perception of sound*, although this is not well understood. Efferent synapses occur on outer hair cells and on afferent (towards the brain) dendrites under inner hair cells

The central auditory system

This sound information, now re-encoded, travels down the *vestibulocochlear nerve*, through intermediate stations such as the *cochlear nuclei* and *superior olivary complex* of the brainstem and the *inferior colliculus* of the midbrain, being further processed at each waypoint. The information eventually reaches the thalamus, and from there it is relayed to the cortex. In the human brain, the primary auditory cortex is located in the *temporal lobe*.

There are associated anatomical structures and these include:

The cochlear nucleus

The *cochlear nucleus* is the first site of the neuronal processing of the newly converted "digital" data from the inner ear. In mammals, this region is anatomically and physiologically split into two regions, the *dorsal cochlear nucleus* and *ventral cochlear nucleus*.

The trapezoid body

The *trapezoid body* is a bundle of decussating (crossing) fibers in the *ventral pons* that carry information used for binaural computations in the brainstem.

The superior olivary complex

The *superior olivary complex* is located in the *pons*, and receives projections predominantly from the *ventral cochlear nucleus*. Within the *superior olivary complex* lies the *lateral superior olive* and the *medial superior olive*.

The lateral lemniscus

The *lateral lemniscus* is a tract of axons in the brainstem that carries information about sound from the *cochlear nucleus* to various brainstem nuclei and ultimately the *contralateral inferior colliculus* of the midbrain

The inferior colliculus

The *inferior colliculus* are located just below the visual processing centers known as the superior colliculi. The central nucleus of the *inferior colliculus* most likely acts to integrate information (specifically regarding sound source localization) from the *superior olivary complex* and *dorsal cochlear nucleus* before sending it to the *thalamus* and *cortex.*

The medial geniculate nucleus

Sensory information enters both the auditory and the limbic systems through the *medial geniculate nucleus,* a small oval mass that protrudes slightly from the underside of the *thalamus,* a large double-lobed structure buried beneath the *cerebral cortex.* Before the signal can travel on, however, it travels through another nearby structure called the *thalamic reticular nucleus,* which evaluates whether or not it should be passed on. Here we have the anatomical structures that are responsible **for filtering out what we determine to be unwanted noises.** If this part of the hearing process determines that the noise is unwanted the *thalamic reticular nucleus* feeds back the information to the *medial geniculate nucleus* and the signal goes no further. **It will not travel on to the auditory cortex.** One can hypothesize that in 4S sufferers, as opposed to other people trigger noises are simply not filtered out as unwanted and actually are mis-processed as signals that are significant, and require a response.(1)

The primary auditory cortex

The *primary auditory cortex* is the first region of *cerebral cortex* to receive auditory input. The auditory cortex is the most highly organized processing unit of sound in the brain. This cortex area is the neural crux of hearing, and in humans of language and music.

Perception of sound is associated with the *left posterior superior temporal gyrus.* The *superior temporal gyrus* contains several important structures of the brain, including *Brodmann areas 41* and *42,* marking the location of the *primary auditory cortex,* the cortical region responsible for the sensation of basic characteristics of sound such as pitch and rhythm.

The *primary auditory cortex* is surrounded by the *secondary auditory cortex*, and interconnects with it. These secondary areas interconnect with further processing areas in the *superior temporal gyrus*, in the dorsal bank of the *superior temporal sulcus*, and in the *frontal lobe*. In humans, connections of these regions with the *middle temporal gyrus* are probably important for speech perception. The *frontotemporal system* underlying auditory perception allows us to distinguish sounds as speech, music, or noise.(2) Damage to the Primary Auditory Cortex in humans leads to a loss of any awareness of sound, but an ability to react reflexively to sounds remains as there is a great deal of subcortical processing in the auditory brainstem and midbrain. The auditory cortex is involved in tasks such as identifying and segregating auditory "objects" and identifying the location of a sound in space. The auditory cortex is an important yet ambiguous part of the hearing process. When the sound pulses pass into the cortex, the specifics of what exactly takes place are unclear.

So as we can see, the process of hearing is extremely complex. And not only does it involve a physical process, but when the stimuli reach our brain what we hear and how we hear it can be influenced by the way that we feel, and interpreted in different ways. With the 4S sufferer the process of interpreting sounds is faulty, and innocent innocuous sounds relating to others, principally eating and breathing, has become linked in the neuronal pathways of the brain to the physiological arousal and emotional centers. Hearing the trigger sounds then leads to a cascade of physiological, emotional and cognitive reactions. As we have said, it is a mystery as to why this occurs. In an evolutionary context it simply does not make sense to react in a negative way to such stimuli, apart from our postulation above that it may be of use in perceiving the sounds of predators who may be about to attack us. To go back to our cave man analogy to hear other people eating and breathing are the very noises of life itself. And sitting in a cave around a fire with people happily engaged in eating food (and breathing!) would mean that life is present and the survival of the species is assured. But this faulty processing is precisely why we refer to 4S as a disorder.

5

How do we cope?

'To manage, people with the condition can employ coping skills such as wearing ear plugs or playing white noise to drown out the trigger sound, according to Misophonia UK. Therapy, including cognitive behavioral therapy and hypnotherapy, is also an option.'(1)

We are all born into life with no preparation for the path ahead. We have in-built survival and coping mechanisms. One of the most primitive of these is the survival strategy of *escape-avoidance*. This is when we wish to escape from, and to avoid, the stimuli that we find obnoxious. It's an ancient mechanism. And we 4S sufferers use it all of the time. The first thing that I will say about this coping strategy is that we can and should use it, if that prevents the build up of rage and possible conflict with others. In some situations we may have a choice and an option to escape the 4S trigger noises. Many of us sufferers eat with others. And when the trigger sounds are too much we have to escape. We have to make do with this basic defense, until we are able to learn other, perhaps more effective coping strategies. In certain situations we have no option, no possibility, of escape. In the cubicle next to a work colleague who is sniffing all day, or on a plane next to someone smacking their lips as they chew on candy. In these situations where we cannot escape, it is use of the ear plugs, or music on headphones, or background music to attenuate the trigger noises. Let me repeat again that there is, as far as I am aware, no cure for 4S. If there is please let me know, as I would myself like to avail of any such therapy! So in the absence of a cure for the condition that can so blight our lives we have to attempt to increase our capacity to cope with it. We may regard coping with life and its travails as the central problem of our existence. As has been said, we all have a cross to bear. Something that makes our lives less that perfect. With phobic disorder there are treatment approaches referred to as *desensitization* and *flooding*. In desensitization the individual is gradually exposed to the phobic object or situation a little at a time. It is graded exposure and it can result in a lessening of the phobic symptoms. In flooding the individual is 'thrown in at the deep end' and exposed immediately, fully and for a prolonged period to the feared object or situation. The human organism can only remain acutely anxious for a relatively short period of time. This is because the surge of hormones, such as *adrenaline* and *noradrenaline* that mediate the fear response, can only be maintained for a limited time. Thus anxiety and fear will peak but then must inevitably subside. For anxiety and phobic disorder we have a huge amount of research and evidence relating to the efficacy of treatments. But as I have already stated the 4S syndrome is not a phobic disorder. It is a clinical entity in its own right. Research needs to be conducted as to whether comparable methods as these would be of benefit in 4S. One of the critical things that is important for us as sufferers, and for relatives too, is to recognize the following:

1) 4S is a clinical syndrome and a condition just like any other. Its sufferers are disadvantaged and suffer great distress, as can their relatives. Avoid blame and recrimination. Deal with it as one would with any other illness.

2) 4S sufferers have no immediate control over the symptoms that they experience. However 4S sufferers are not psychotic, they for the most part do not have diminished responsibility, and therefore are fully responsible for their own behavior and the consequences of their behavior.

3) There is no known cure for the clinical condition of 4S. Certain strategies to assist coping may well help. One of the most important of these is to seek support and communication with other sufferers. Join one of the support networks that are listed in the resources section of this handbook. Ask your relatives to join too. This is important to help us as sufferers, and to allow to others understand what we are going through and for them to receive support too.

4) Engage in general stress reduction strategies. Exercise, eat well, (alone or with others!), take time out for hobbies and having fun, maintain supportive relationships.

5) If you suffer from 4S *be upfront* about that with relatives, friends and colleagues. You will find that you are not the only one to suffer from the condition. Some of them may do so too! If things are bad at home or at work speak to the individuals concerned. In private with them say something like:

'I suffer from a condition called 4S. It's an illness that makes me get really annoyed about certain noises and sounds that people make. Please forgive me if I appear irritated or angry at times, it's not my fault and it's not your fault. It's just that when people (sniff, smack their lips,

chew gum) I really cringe and it irritates me badly. I do my best to control it, but I may have bad days so I would really appreciate your support and your help with this.'

If the person so addressed is a good friend and a good colleague they will understand and support you.

6) Always seek balance in your life. Spend time with people and time away from them, to recharge your batteries.

7) Structure your life so that you are as exposed to trigger noises as little as possible. If you find yourself exceedingly stressed by eating with your family arrange your work or schedule so that you arrive home just after they have finished eating. Explain to them that your work schedule prevents you from being home any earlier. It is fine to eat on your own. Do not overwhelm yourself with stress. You are being avoidant, but if the alternative is to feel tortured at meal times, to get angry with your family and to make life miserable, then choose avoidance! Be easy on yourself and others. Avoid confrontation, it will likely not resolve anything and just make things worse.

In Chapter 3 above we mentioned that the 4S sufferer experiences the symptoms on three levels, the physical, (*I really squirm, feel uncomfortable, want to escape etc.*), the emotional, (*I get so angry, upset, furious, cry etc*), and the cognitive, (*I just imagine hitting him, killing her, they do it on purpose to annoy me, etc.*). It may be useful to plan interventions aimed at calming, redirecting and reframing the response on the 3 separate levels. It would be of general benefit and possibly of specific help in regards to 4S to practice relaxation and meditation. What we may achieve by this is to dampen and control the arousal level of our autonomic nervous system, so that we become physiologically less reactive. We can never diminish completely our physiological arousal mechanisms, and neither should we, as they are essential protective mechanisms that prepare us to deal with real danger. But we can achieve a *'relaxation response'*. This response, which is the result of training ourselves to relax, was formulated by Dr. Herbert Benson(2). It may well prove useful as a tool in the armory of 4S sufferers to assist in managing the condition. Secondly, on the emotional level, again we are human beings and we cannot stop feeling and reacting to things emotionally. But what we may try to do is to *modify* our emotional responses. Meditation can be very useful in this regards in terms of recognizing our emotions and the power that they exert over us. 'To cultivate detachment, a separation from all this, to view the world as less enticing and less permanent, to be detached from its pain...... Cultivating this sort of detachment is as if you are holding the world at arms length slightly and looking askance at it.'(3) From that we can move on to the process of obtaining some sense of detachment from emotional responses that are maladaptive. On the cognitive level we sometimes worsen the intensity of the emotional and physical reactions by the negative cognitions that we have. So we may say for instance, in our heads, *this person is making these noises deliberately. They are just a pig. They are just doing that to annoy me.* We need to restructure and reframe our perceptions, these cognitions, because they can make us feel and think and react more intensely to how we might otherwise react. As 4S sufferers we might instead say,

That person is really starting to annoy me. If I am able to do so I will remove myself from this situation if I start to feel overwhelmed. Or I will just put in my ear plugs or use my headphones. I have some control here.

I am a 4S sufferer and so it is part of the way that I am made that makes me feel this way. I will be easy on myself and this other person.

I will not devalue this person, they are a human being.

The noises that they are making are harmless. This person does not wish to harm me.

This feeling of anger and annoyance will pass. Feelings are temporary.

There is no specific pharmacotherapy, or medicines, that are available as specific treatment for 4S. If you suffer from anxiety or depression in addition to 4S then your doctor may initiate specific treatment to deal with this. It is advisable to find a doctor, audiologist, health professional or counselor who can discuss with you your symptoms, assess and monitor your condition, and formulate with you an intervention plan.

There is no reason why a 4S sufferer cannot be a winner in life. We suffer from a condition that can cause us great distress; however we can take measures to help us cope. And we can still listen to the works of Beethoven and Vivaldi, hear the birds singing their sweet melody in the trees, and thereby get a sense of the miracle of life and the universe.

Support

Supports, Support Organizations and Websites

The first person to see if 4S symptoms are bothersome:
- Your Family Physician / General Practitioner
- Your local Audiologist

Other supports:
- Your local Community Health Center which may have courses on relaxation, self-development, self-esteem and life skills.

Websites
- www.soundsensitive.org
- www.tinnitus-audiology.com
- www.misophonia-uk.org
- www.health.groups.yahoo.com/group/Soundsensitivity
- www.relaxationresponse.org
- www.hyperacusis.org

References

Introduction

(1)   http://en.allexperts.com/q/Phobias-3097/f/Unable-tolerate-chewing-smacking.htm)

(2)   Ibid.

(3)   http://www.advancedrenaleducation.com/GeneralTopics/BasicStatistics/Incidenceandprevalence/tabid/520/Default.aspx

Chapter 1

(1)   http://www.tinnitus-audiology.com/softsound.html

(2)   Wikipedia

(3)   http://www.hyperacusis.org

(4)   Wikipedia

(5)   Ibid.

(6)   Ibid.

(7)   Ibid.

(8)   Ibid.

(9)   www.hyperacusis.org

(10)   Ibid.

(11)   http://medical-dictionary.thefreedictionary.com/Phobias

(12)   http://biology.about.com/od/anatomy/p/Amygdala.htm

(13)   www.hyperacusis.org

(14)   http://medical-dictionary.thefreedictionary.com/nosology

(15)   Wikipedia

(16)   Paul Wolf, Clinical professor of pathology. University of California. www.ncbi.nlm.nih.gov/pmc/articles/PMC1071597

Chapter 2

(1) http://www.medilexicon.com
(2) http://www.medterms.com

Chapter 3

(1) http://en.allexperts.com/q/Phobias-3097/f/Unable-tolerate-chewing-smacking.htm
(2) Ibid.
(3) Mosby's Medical Dictionary, 8th edition.
(4) http://soundsensitive.org
(5) Wikipedia
(6) Ibid.
(7) http://en.allexperts.com/q/Phobias-3097/f/Unable-tolerate-chewing-smacking.htm
(8) http://medical-dictionary.thefreedictionary.com/phenomenological+research
(9) The Telegraph Online. www.telegraph.co.uk, 21st February, 2011, and at www.dailyrecord.co.uk.

Chapter 4

The anatomy and physiology of hearing
(1) http://www.nidcd.nih.gov/news/releases/11/pages/031611.aspx
(2) Wikipedia

Chapter 5

How do we cope?
(1) www.huffingtonpost.com/2011/09/08/misophonia-annoying-noises-disorder_n_953892.html
(2) http://www.relaxationresponse.org/steps
(5) http://www.homeoint.org/morrell/buddhism/nonatt.html

Personal Notes

Made in the USA
Lexington, KY
27 January 2014